Music by Luke Bedford
Words by Glyn Maxwell

Performances 2011

17, 18 June CBSO Centre Birmingham, WORLD PREMIERE

20 June Bute Theatre, Royal Welsh College of Music & Drama, Cardiff

28, 29 June Tramway, Glasgow

3 July Brighton Dome – Corn Exchange

8 July Oxford Playhouse

12, 14, 15 July Linbury Studio Theatre, Royal Opera House, London

16 July Latitude Festival, Suffolk

The Opera Group and BCMG production, co-produced with ROH2 and Tramway.

www.theoperagroup.co.uk
www.bcmg.org.uk

Running time about 1hour 45 minutes including interval

Welcome to Seven Angels

Five years ago we sat down to talk about how a collaboration between us might sound. We each arrived at a meeting with a wish-list of the composers we most wanted to commission. The meeting was short because Luke Bedford sat at the top of both our lists.

When Luke had identified Glyn Maxwell as the librettist he would work with, they wrote a concert work for BCMG which took a moment in Milton's *Paradise Lost* as its starting point. *Good Dream She Has* was premiered in Birmingham in 2008.

After completing the concert work, we took Luke and Glyn to visit Wakehurst Place, Kew Garden's outpost which houses the millennium seedbank, where a combination of edenic gardens and a pessimistic futurologist challenged us all to see Milton's ecology in a new light. Then we watched as Luke and Glyn's shared fascination with Milton, with language and with the retelling of tales shaped a piece which has the weight of myth and yet which could only have been made now. They talked about exploding the Milton and constructing a new story from the shards.

And then the conversation exploded too. BCMG has a long history of collaborating with Jonathan Watkins at Ikon. Through Jonathan we met Japanese artist Tadasu Takamine who has not only designed the opera, but also has a concurrent exhibition at Ikon Gallery this summer. Our partnerships with our co-producers at ROH2 at the Royal Opera House and Tramway Glasgow have been essential to making the production happen. And our collaboration with Friends of the Earth has given birth to a sister opera which will tour outdoors alongside *Seven Angels*. We are grateful also to the many funding partners and donors who have supported the development, commissioning, producing and touring of the project.

Collaboration is a creative necessity – we are at our best when in conversation with each other, with artists and with audiences. Welcome to the conversation – we look forward to hearing what you think.

John Fulljames
Artistic Director
The Opera Group

Stephen Newbould
Artistic Director
Birmingham Contemporary
Music Group

Seven Angels was commissioned and produced by The Opera Group and Birmingham Contemporary Music Group and co-produced with ROH2 and Tramway Glasgow. Commissioned with funds generously provided by the John Feeney Charitable Trust, the opera was developed with the support of a Jerwood Opera Fellowship at Aldeburgh Music and the Columbia Foundation Fund of the Capital Community Foundation.

The Opera Group is grateful to the following individuals for their support of *Seven Angels:*

David Bernstein, Robin Bidwell, Geoffrey Collens, Peter Espenhahn, Ian Hamilton, John Hughes, Thomas Lingard, Peter Lofthouse, Robert McFarland, Anthony Newhouse and Virginia Rushton.

BCMG is grateful to the following individuals for their support of *Seven Angels*:

Viv and Hazel Astling, Paul and Jean Bacon, William and Jane Barry, Paul Bond, Christopher Carrier, John Christophers, Alan Cook, Anne P Fletcher, Barrie Gavin, Richard Hartree, Tessa and Charles King-Farlow, Jeremy Lindon, Elizabeth Robinson for the Rowan Trust, Carolyn and Richard Sugden, Janet Waterhouse, Elizabeth and Barrie Withers; BCMG Foundation members: Kiaran Asthana, Alan S Carr, Alan Cook, Bernard Samuels, John and Anne Sweet; and two donors wishing to remain anonymous.

We are grateful to the following funders for their support of *Seven Angels:*

Arts Council England, Arts & Business, Daiwa Foundation, D'Oyly Carte Charitable Trust, Colwinston Charitable Trust, Esmée Fairbairn Foundation, Great Britain Sasakawa Foundation, Japan Foundation, Jerwood Space, Leche Trust, Reed Foundation, RVW Trust and funding through Beyond Borders from the PRS for Music Foundation, Creative Scotland, Arts Council Northern Ireland, Arts Council Wales and Foyle Foundation.

Seven Angels

Music by Luke Bedford
Words by Glyn Maxwell

Angel 1 / Waitress	Rhona McKail
Angel 2 /Queen	Emma Selway
Angel 3 / Chef / Priestess	Louise Mott
Angel 4 / Prince	Christopher Lemmings
Angel 5 / Porter / Industrialist	Joseph Shovelton
Angel 6 / Gardener / General	Owen Gilhooly
Angel 7 / King	Keel Watson

BCMG Players

Flute / Piccolo / Alto Flute	Marie-Christine Zupancic
Clarinet / Bass Clarinet	Mark O'Brien
Bassoon / Contra-bassoon	Margaret Cookhorn
Trumpet / Flugelhorn	Jonathan Holland
Trombone	Duncan Wilson
Percussion	Simon Limbrick
Piano	Malcolm Wilson
Viola 1	Christopher Yates
Viola 2	Michael Jenkinson
Viola 3	Myriam Guillaume
Viola 4 / Violin	Marcus Barcham-Stevens
Double Bass	John Tattersdill

Conductor	Nicholas Collon
Director	John Fulljames
Designer	Tadasu Takamine
Lighting	Jon Clark
Projection	Ian William Galloway
Movement Director	Sandra Maturana
Repetiteur	John-Paul Gandy
Casting Consultant	Sarah Playfair
Production Manager	Cath Bates
Company Stage Manager	Rupert Carlile
Deputy Stage Manager	Jennifer Llewellyn
Assistant Stage Manager	Michelle Thomas
Costume Supervisor	Yoko Yamano
Technical Stage Manager	Micky Fernandez
Tour Lighting	Peter Harrison, Mim Spencer
AV Technician	Salvador Avila
Wardrobe Supervisor	Morag Hood

Additional thanks:

Better World Books, Big Give, Bob & Elisabeth Boas, Pete Foggitt, Rachel Gimber, Guildhall School of Music & Drama, Sophie Henstridge, King's College London, Chelsea Lawrence, Thomas Lingard, James Longford, Niki Longhurst, Sherry Neyhus, Oberon Books, Jonathan Reekie, Faye Scott and Green Alliance, Wakehurst Place, Kew Gardens, Jonathan Watkins and Ikon Gallery, Joanna Watson and Friends of the Earth, Weil, Gotshal & Manges.

Tadasu Takamine
Too far to see
4 May – 17 July 2011
Ikon Gallery, 1 Oozells Square, Brindleyplace,
Birmingham B1 2HS
www.ikon-gallery.co.uk / 0121 248 0708
Free Entry

Paradise Lost

Milton's *Paradise Lost* provided a starting point for a meditation on the relationship between humanity and the resources of the earth. Where the great poem is a symphonic retelling of scripture, *Seven Angels* was grown from fragments, shards of the poem, as if that huge incandescent structure had toppled from its seat in heaven and shattered into glimpses, dreams, strange tales, lost threads, all strewn across a broken landscape.

In the world of *Paradise Lost*, we know the story, we know the outcome, we know what Milton intends: the glorious pentameters sound the inevitability of the Devils' fall from Heaven, Man's fall from Eden, the Redemption through Christ. *Seven Angels* grows in a world without inevitability, without known story or outcome, with forms and rhythms that slide and mutate, with causes unclear and effects unknown. This world.

Glyn Maxwell

The Story

Seven figures find themselves on a desert, having dropped out of the sky. They are angels, abandoned by God, forgotten by Satan, passed over by Milton, fallen out of history. They have fallen for so long they no longer know who punished them, who they are, where they are, or why. The land is scorched and barren, the air thick with poison. Shadows war perpetually on every horizon.

They think they hear a creature, crying on the wind. They wonder – is it looking for us? In panic, the seven try to piece together a story to make sense of what has happened in this place. They make a series of rapid deductions: if the creature is crying, there must have been a better time, a beautiful past, when the desert was a garden. The story gains its own momentum as the figures transform themselves into characters...

> In the Garden there lives a King and a Queen, and they give birth to a Prince. They love the Prince so much that they give him whatever he desires. They feed him the fruits of the Garden, and they are served by a Royal Household.

> Word of the Garden is carried around the world on the wind. In time, out of lands ravaged by famine, war, and tyranny, three delegates travel towards the Garden seeking plenty, peace, and mercy. The King and Queen, wishing to keep the delights of the Garden to themselves, close its gates.

The Household, exhausted by the demands of the spoiled Prince, the closure of the Garden, and the failing of the palace stores, start quitting, one by one, leaving only an exhausted Waitress. The Prince notices the Waitress for the first time, and falls in love with her. She persuades him that they must re-open the Garden, in order to feed the people beyond the gates of the palace.

The King chairs a summit meeting, as the three Delegates arrive from their desperate homelands, one ruined by industrial despoliation, one by war, and one by fanaticism. They plead for help from the King and his Garden, as the Waitress serves them the last three meals in the world. As the food runs out, the Delegates discover that the Garden is itself a wasteland, and the Queen's belief in 'an infinity of plenty' a delusion that science will save the earth somehow.

The story collapses along with the hope that the Garden represented. The characters dissolve back into angels falling through space – but two of them remember their story, believe in it, and refuse to abandon the world. The Prince and the Waitress leave the palace and head out into the desert, to join the nameless, numberless folk beyond the gates.

Milton and Ecology

Seven Angels takes up what is perhaps the most important theme in Milton's *Paradise Lost*. Like many Renaissance thinkers, Milton believed that the decisive event in human history was the biblical Fall, the moment when sin and death were released into the world. In fact, Sin and Death, whom Satan must both recognize and overcome in order to reach Eden, are wonderfully (and hideously) personified in *Paradise Lost*. Nonetheless, while they make an appearance in Milton's epic, the poet is not primarily interested in exploring, as were many biblical commentators of his day, the story of sin's discovery or death's release into the world. Instead, he takes up a third, often ignored, consequence of the Fall: not only was Eden lost as a result of human folly, but the entire earth suffered as well because, as many theologians believed, our planet is in a state of decay because of Original Sin. Consequently, from his title onward, Milton considers the tragic story of *Paradise lost*.

Milton lived in an environmentally decisive time and place: early modern London. Scores of distinctly modern environmental problems either emerged or mushroomed in this period. For example, by the decade that *Paradise Lost* was published, it was already known that respiratory disease caused by the wholesale burning of a particularly dangerous, highly sulfurous coal ("sea-coal," which Glyn Maxwell references in his libretto) was quickly becoming a leading cause of human deaths in London. It was also known at the time to be killing plants and animals, as well as even eating away the surfaces of stone buildings. Faced with a range of similarly modern environmental issues, seventeenth-century thinkers rekindled what had previously been something of an arcane theological issue: If human beings are fallen as a result of Original Sin, and Paradise was lost through the act, what about the rest of the planet? In Christian thinking, human beings are, of course, able to be saved, but in Milton's time it was often assumed – as it is still today by some Christian thinkers – that the entire Earth was in a state of irretrievable decay as a result of the Fall. Obviously, this has profound environmental consequences, as there is little reason to care about (or for) a planet that cannot be saved.

Milton, himself a careful Christian thinker, strongly disagreed with this last sentiment, as he believed that human beings could remedy at least one of the consequences of the Fall by helping the planet to regenerate after the apocalypse brought about by Adam and Eve. To our modern sensibilities, it might seem strange to think of Milton as a post-apocalyptic thinker; nonetheless, like most individuals in Renaissance England, he believed that an epoch-making event, the act of Original Sin, had forever changed the earth. Consequently, the planet on which we live, with its many problems and afflictions, is not a "natural" one at all, but the result of human folly. To Milton, while we cannot turn back the clock and undo Original Sin, we can, nonetheless, work to return the earth to its natural state before the Fall. While the underlying rationale may be different, this thinking has obvious and profound similarities with very constructive modern environmental arguments, as both approaches acknowledge human beings as the cause of environmental problems, as well as (let's hope) their cure.

Like *Paradise Lost*, which in part inspired Maxwell's libretto, *Seven Angels* considers the earth as a post-apocalyptic garden. What is striking about considering *Paradise Lost* and *Seven Angels*, which are separated by nearly 350 years, together is that the question of our relationship to the planet is still a timely one. In fact, it is more so now than ever. Both *Seven Angels* and *Paradise Lost* end with the dawn of a new era. In Milton's epic, Adam and Eve, "hand in hand, with wandering steps and slow, / Through Eden took their solitary way" out of Paradise and into an uncertain future. *Seven Angels* ends as Maxwell's reinscription of the pair, "the Prince and the Waitress," see signs of survivors in a desolate landscape, and "hand in hand they set off towards them." The question facing both Milton's and Maxwell's protagonists is the same one facing us all today: What next? Do we give up on our planet as lost, or do we, as Milton suggests, work to undo our folly by taking upon ourselves the task of regenerating Paradise?

Professor Ken Hiltner, author of "Milton and Ecology".

Insight Activities

Alongside the main stage production of *Seven Angels*, The Opera Group has been working in collaboration with Friends of the Earth to create a complementary series of activities exploring the issues from the opera.

These include:

- A street opera by composer Julian Philips and writer Simon Christmas and directed by Sasha Milavic Davies – *Save the Diva* – that visited five cities in the run up to *Seven Angels*
- A project for emerging composers and writers
- Pre and post-show debates featuring environmental experts and the *Seven Angels* creative team

Save the Diva was performed guerrilla-style on the streets on Cardiff, Birmingham, Brighton, Glasgow and London. Two spectacularly outrageous divas defended their right to consume as much of the planet's resources as possible through their 'Save the Diva' campaign, only for their put-upon servant to see the error of their ways and sabotage their campaign.

In April, 28 emerging composers and writers took part in a masterclass examining the collaborative process of writing opera. From those participants two went on to receive intensive mentoring, culminating in the creation of a new mini-opera – Is This It? – exploring the same themes as *Seven Angels*, to be performed at the Royal Opera House on 14 July.

Is This It? addresses the issues of individual action and personal responsibility, this new opera by Liz Johnson and Rosalind Haslett is a companion piece to *Seven Angels*. When an extra angel appears in the foyer of the opera house the management are thrown into confusion – and it soon becomes apparent that this is no ordinary angel. One man must take action to save the theatre, the audience, the earth – not to mention the heavens – from the angel in the foyer.

For more information on these Insight Activities visit www.theoperagroup.co.uk.

We are grateful to the European Commission Representation in the UK for their support of *Save the Diva*.

EUROPEAN COMMISSION
Representation in the UK

**Friends of
the Earth**

Bringing together art and activism has created some of the most exciting and relevant work of the last century. Friends of the Earth is proud to be part of that tradition by partnering with The Opera Group and BCMG in support of *Seven Angels* and street opera *Save the Diva*.

We are an environmental campaigning charity, bringing people together to put pressure on politicians to ensure they make the fairest decisions for everyone. We have been making things happen since 1971 – from our own back yard to the global stage. We've campaigned on a huge number of important green issues, from saving the rainforests to recycling, to tackling climate change.

Over our 40 year history, we've helped ban whale hunting, won victories against nuclear expansion in the UK and brought doorstep recycling to UK homes. Our Big Ask campaign brought together hundreds of thousands of people to persuade the Government to bring in the Climate Change Act, a world first law setting legal limits on the UK's emissions of greenhouse gases.

Now we're putting pressure on the Government to ensure their top energy priority is investment in renewable power and slashing energy waste in homes and businesses.

The themes explored in *Seven Angels* are also reflected in our vision of a fairer, safer world – now and in the future. We hope you agree that the ravaged and over-exploited planet portrayed by *Seven Angels* is one we should work hard to avoid.

Friends of the Earth is about making your voice count. You can take action by:

Joining a Friends of the Earth local group. Find out more at www.foe.co.uk/actlocal

Adding your voice to our climate campaigns at www.foe.co.uk

Donating to Friends of the Earth – more than 90 per cent of our income comes from individuals, so we rely on donations to continue our vital work.

Find out more at www.foe.co.uk or email savethediva@foe.co.uk.

We have 230 local groups in the UK, and we are also part of Friends of the Earth International, a federation of 77 environmental groups across the world.

the◯peragroup

The Opera Group tours music theatre across the UK and internationally – re-creating rarely performed gems and commissioning fresh new works from artists of the future. Inspired by the rapidly changing world around us, the starting point for everything we do is discovery – identifying great stories and discovering new ways to tell those stories to our ever changing audience. We actively seek to work in partnership with other ideas-led organisations to spread the conversations generated by our work.

We work in collaboration with a wide variety of partners including producing theatres, ensembles, education bodies and non-arts organisations to deliver a range of different projects which include touring work, projects for children & family audiences, site specific work and participatory projects for young people. Our partners share our passion for reaching the widest possible audience.

We work in association with a range of producing theatres including the Young Vic, Anvil Arts Basingstoke, Brighton Dome & Festival, Oxford Playhouse and Watford Palace Theatre and regularly visit and co-produce with ROH2 at the Royal Opera House. The Opera Group is currently in residence at King's College London.

Artistic Director John Fulljames
Executive Producer Patrick Dickie
General Manager Alison Porter
Insight Programme Manager Nina Swann
Development Manager Rebecca Redclift
Creative Associate Michelle Thomas
Company Assistant Nicole Samuels
Press and PR Faith Wilson Arts Publicity
Marketing Ben Jefferies for makesthree
Finance Allison Rosser, Sandra Francis-Love
Trustees Claudia Pendred (chair), David Bernstein, John Gilhooly, Lindsey Glen, Paul Kearney, Alice King-Farlow, Anthony Newhouse, Andrew Newman

The Opera Group
23-SWB King's College London, The Strand, London, WC2R 2LS
020 7848 7314 / enquiries@theoperagroup.co.uk / www.theoperagroup.co.uk

The Opera Group is a company limited by guarantee registered in England No. 3508706
Registered Charity No. 1070013 VAT No. 749404416

Become an OperaGroupie!

The OperaGroupies are key supporters of The Opera Group. For as little as £100 a year anyone can become an OperaGroupie and gain an insight into the development of a new opera.

Join the OperaGroupies for as little as £100 a year and enjoy the following benefits:

- Meet the cast, and each other, and see the difference your contribution makes at private model showings, exclusive presentations and open rehearsals.
- Purchase tickets to exclusive opening night performances and post-show parties.
- Stay in touch with developing new work and forthcoming shows with The Opera Group's quarterly newsletter.
- Acknowledgement of your support in our programmes and on our website.

For those who wish to become involved with specific aspects of our productions, we offer tailored opportunities around specific productions including for example:

- One singer for one performance for £250
- An orchestral rehearsal for £500
- Costumes for a new production for £7,000
- Commission of a new opera for £20,000

The OperaGroupies:

John and June Bedford, David Bernstein, Sherban Cantacuzino, Albert Edwards, John Fox, John Gilhooly, Ian Hamilton, David Howie, Robert and Lindsey Kaye, Thomas Lingard, Robert McFarland, Ryan Myint, Andy Newman, Sherry Neyhus, Marie-Hélène Osterweil Cohen, Claudia Pendred, Ed Ross, Virginia Rushton, Ellen Solomon, Peter Toye, Sir John Tusa, Nick Walden, Christian Wells.

How to join the Groupies:

Call Rebecca Redclift on 020 7848 7314 or email rebeccaredclift@theoperagroup.co.uk

The Opera Group is grateful to the following for their support of our work in 2010/11:

Major Donors:

Robin Bidwell, Anthony Bolton, Anthony Bunker, Geoffrey Collens, Vernon Ellis, Peter Espenhahn, Ian Hamilton, John Hughes, Thomas Lingard, Peter Lofthouse, Robert McFarland, Anthony Newhouse, Alan Rusbridger, Virginia Rushton, David M. Wells.

Supporters:

Anonymous, Arts & Business, Arts Council England, Columbia Foundation Fund of the Capital Community Foundation, John S Cohen Foundation, Colwinston Charitable Trust, Daiwa Foundation, Department for Culture, Media and Sport, The D'Oyly Carte Charitable Trust, The Eranda Foundation, The Ellerman Foundation, Esmée Fairbairn Foundation, European Commission Representation in the UK, Fidelio Charitable Trust, Fidelity UK Foundation, Garfield Weston Foundation, Golsoncott Foundation, Great Britain Sasakawa Foundation, Japan Foundation, Jerwood Charitable Foundation, Jerwood Space, Leche Trust, The Linbury Trust, The Mercers' Company, The Peter Moores Foundation, Pro Helvetia, PRS for Music Foundation, Reed Foundation, The RVW Trust, N Smith Charitable Trust, Thistle Trust, The Wellcome Trust.

Birmingham Contemporary Music Group

BCMG was formed in 1987 from within the City of Birmingham Symphony Orchestra and is established as one of Europe's leading ensembles. Sir Simon Rattle is BCMG's Founding Patron and the Group has Oliver Knussen, John Woolrich and Peter Wiegold as Artists-in-Association.

The core of BCMG's work is the commissioning and performance of new music. The Group has premiered some 140 new works by leading UK and overseas composers and has given over 530 performances of these pieces. Most have been commissioned with the help of a large number of individuals through BCMG's ground-breaking Sound Investment scheme.

The Group regularly tours nationally and internationally and UK engagements include regular appearances at the BBC Proms and at the Aldeburgh Festival – in 2011 giving the world premiere of *Conversations* by Elliott Carter conducted by Oliver Knussen.

2011/12 brings concerts with Oliver Knussen celebrating the composer's 60th birthday, in Birmingham and at the Aldeburgh Festival; more ground-breaking Family Concerts; and the UK premiere performances of Gerald Barry's concert opera *The Importance of Being Earnest* at London's Barbican and Symphony Hall, Birmingham conducted by Thomas Adès.

BCMG's work has won several major awards including a MIDEM award for the NMC recording of Britten's complete film music; two Royal Philharmonic Society Awards; Prudential, Gramophone and PRS Millennial awards.

BCMG Learning

BCMG is passionate about involving young people and the wider community in the performance and creation of new music. Projects take place in schools, in higher education, in the community and in our home the CBSO Centre, and are run by BCMG musicians, workshop leaders, composers and conductors of the highest calibre. We have a full programme of out-of-school hours composing and creative music-making workshops for young people from age 8-18 encompassing *Music Maze*, the *Zigzag Ensemble* and *Feel the Buzz* running throughout the season.

Music Maze is a series of creative, participatory workshops which take place at weekends and are linked to music from BCMG's concerts. On 5 June, *Music Maze* participants (aged 8-11) created their own opera exploring the theme of the environment and climate change.

To hear these Music Maze operas and for more information about BCMG, please visit **www.bcmg.org.uk**

Sound Investment – Share in music's future

Sound Investment is BCMG's pioneering commissioning scheme, which involves individuals in the thrill of bringing alive new work by the most exciting composers of our time.

Join our extended family of Sound Investors and you can:
- attend rehearsals and premieres
- meet composers and performers
- have your name listed in a new work's score

Sound Unit shares in each commission are priced at £150. You can currently invest in commissions by Silvina Milstein, Param Vir, Colin Matthews, Benedict Mason, Harrison Birtwistle and David Lang.

To find out more please contact Gwendolyn Tietze on 0121 616 2616 or email gwendolyn@bcmg.org.uk.

www.bcmg.org.uk/soundinvestment

We at BCMG would like to thank our charitable trust supporters and individual donors for their generous support during this season.

ROYAL
OPERA
HOUSE

Tramway is an international art-space that commissions, produces and presents contemporary art projects and programmes. Tramway's vision is to inspire and add value to our understanding of today's world by connecting artists and audiences. Tramway is a space where everyone is welcomed to witness, engage, experience, participate, be challenged and learn.

JOHN FEENEY
CHARITABLE TRUST

John Feeney (1839 – 1907) was a prominent Birmingham citizen and a keen supporter of the Arts. He is best known as the founder of the Birmingham Daily Mail and the proprietor of the Birmingham Daily Post and the Birmingham Weekly Post. In his Will, amongst other charitable bequests, Feeney directed that a 9/90th part of his residuary estate was to be held in trust and the income arising used to benefit "any one or more of the public charities in the City of Birmingham, or for the promotion and cultivation of art in the City of Birmingham, or for the acquisition and maintenance of parks, recreation grounds and open spaces in or near the City". Trustees give priority to applications that are about the arts, heritage and open spaces. They have a special interest in encouraging new work in the arts and are well known for nearly fifty Feeney Commissions for the City of Birmingham Symphony Orchestra, several of them now part of the repertoire.

Luke Bedford *Composer*

Luke Bedford was born in 1978 and studied composition at the Royal College of Music with Edwin Roxburgh and Simon Bainbridge. His works range from chamber groups (e.g. the string quartet *Of the Air*), to ensemble, sometimes with voice (*Good Dream She Has* and *Or Voit Tout En Aventure*) and to full orchestra (*Outblaze the Sky*, *Wreathe*). Tom Service wrote of *Or Voit Tout en Aventure*, that is was "one of the most outstanding pieces by any young composer I've ever experienced – music of brooding expressive intensity and charged with that indefinable quality that makes a piece sound as if it was written out of sheer necessity." Bedford was recently the recipient of a prestigious Paul Hamlyn Artists' Award, and in 2008 *Wreathe* won a British Composer Award. 2010 saw the world premiere of *At Three and Two* by the Hallé Orchestra. Bedford is currently the first ever composer in residence at the Wigmore Hall in London. Forthcoming commissions include works for both the Britten Sinfonia and the Scottish Ensemble. *Seven Angels* continues Bedford's fascination with the work of John Milton, as seen previously in works such as *On Time* for choir and orchestra, and *Rode with Darkness* for orchestra.
www.universaledition.com/bedford

Glyn Maxwell *Writer*

Glyn Maxwell's libretti for The Opera Group include *The Lion's Face* (2010) and *The Girl of Sand* (2004) both for Elena Langer and *The Birds* (2005) for Edward Dudley Hughes. *The Firework Maker's Daughter*, based on a Philip Pullman story, is in development with David Bruce. He is working with Graham Fitkin and the LCO on *Track to Track*, one of the twenty 12-minute pieces commissioned for the Olympics. He has won several awards for his poetry, including the Geoffrey Faber Memorial Prize for *The Nerve*, and the E.M. Forster Award from the American Academy of Arts and Letters. *Hide Now* was shortlisted for both the T.S. Eliot and Forward Prizes, and his *One Thousand Nights and Counting: Selected Poems* was published this spring. His plays include *The Lifeblood* (British Theatre Guide's 'Best Play', Edinburgh Fringe 2004), *Liberty* (which premiered at Shakespeare's Globe in 2008), and *The Only Girl in the World* (Time Out Critics' Choice, 2008). His comedy *Merlin and the Woods of Time* is staged this summer as part of the new outdoor season at Grosvenor Park in Chester.
www.steinplays.com

COMPANY BIOGRAPHIES

Rhona McKail *Angel 1 / Waitress*
Rhona McKail, student of John Evans, studied at the Royal Scottish
Academy of Music & Drama and at the Guildhall School of Music &
Drama, where she completed her training on the opera course in 2009.
She has sung the roles of: Anne Trulove in *The Rake's Progress*; Gianetta
in *L'Elisir d'Amore*; Lisette (cover) in *La Rondine* all for British Youth
Opera; Rezia in *La Rencontre Imprévue* – Gluck; Anne Who Steals in *The
King goes forth to France* – Sallinen; Agafya in *The Marriage* – Martinů,
all for GSMD opera; Ortensia (cover) in *Mirandolin* – Martinů for
Garsington Opera; Adele in *Die Fledermaus*; Constance in *The Sorcerer*
and Josephine in *HMS Pinafore* for Opera Della Luna; Fiordiligi in
Cosi fan Tutte for Vignette Productions; and most recently Servillia in
La Clemenza di Tito for English Touring Opera. Rhona has recorded
Messiaen's *La Mort du Nombre* with Sholto Kynoch and *Kaoru Yamada*
for Stone Records and recently performed a recital of contemporary
music in the Purcell Room for the Park Lane Group.

Emma Selway *Angel 2 /Queen*
Emma Selway studied at the Royal Academy of Music and the
National Opera Studio. Roles include Hippolyta (ROH), Kate
Pinkerton, Charlotte *Die Soldaten*, Octavian, Fox *The Cunning Little
Vixen,* Waltraute *The Valkyrie* (ENO), Pauline *Queen of Spades* (WNO),
Sesto *La Clemenza di Tito* (GTO), Musician *Manon Lescaut*, Cephisa
Ermione (Glyndebourne Festival Opera), Dorabella (Opera North,
GTO), Idamante *Idomeneo* (Toronto/Belfast), Carmen (ETO), Anna
Seven Deadly Sins (Batignano), Judith *Duke Bluebeard's Castle* (The Opera
Group), Madame in the world première of John Lunn's *The Maids*
(Lyric, Hammersmith), and Goehr's *Kantan and Damask Drum* (Almeida
Opera/Aldeburgh Festival/Paris). Concerts include *Le Martyre de
St Sébastiane* (Hallé Orchestra), *Seven Sacraments* (Brighton Festival),
Mahler's *Symphony No 2* (Jersey), Mahler's *Symphony No 8* (RPO at the
Royal Albert Hall), Mozart's *Mass in C minor* (London Mozart Players),
the British premiere of Bacalov's *Misa Tango* (Barbican) and Britten's
Spring Symphony and Verdi *Requiem* with the Guinness Choir in Dublin.

Louise Mott *Angel 3 / Chef / Priestess*

Louise Mott's major operatic roles have included Bradamante *Alcina* (ENO), Annio *La Clemenza di Tito* (WNO), Annina *Der Rosenkavalier* and Fidalma *Il matrimonio segreto* (Opera North), the title role in Ariodante (ETO), Madame Larina (Scottish Opera), Katarina Schratt *Mayerling* for the Royal Ballet at The Royal Opera House, Meg Page *Falstaff* (Pfalztheater Kaiserslautern and Diva Opera) and *Alcina, Agrippina, Orlando, Serse,* Sesto *Giulio Cesare* and Dido *Dido and Aeneas* for the Early Opera Company. She has a strong interest in contemporary opera and has already sung Blind Mary *The Martyrdom of St Magnus,* Penelope *Linen from Smyrna* and Emerald *Boys and Girls Come out to Play* for The Opera Group. She has also sung Wife/Sphinx/Doreen *Greek* with the London Sinfonietta and several roles for Almeida Opera and Tête à Tête. Louise made her BBC Proms debut in Vaughan Williams' *Serenade to Music* and has been an oratorio soloist with many of the most important orchestras in the UK.

Christopher Lemmings *Angel 4 / Prince*

The British tenor studied at the Guildhall School of Music & Drama. Recent appearances include ROH Covent Garden, ENO, Glyndebourne, Amsterdam, Madrid, Staatsoper Berlin, Nantes, Strasbourg, Paris, Helsinki, Verona and Los Angeles, under leading conductors including Sir Simon Rattle, Riccardo Muti, Kenneth Montgomery, Sir Colin Davis, Leif Segerstam and Edo de Waart. Recent and future highlights include Bob Boles *Peter Grimes,* Der Bucklige *Die Frau ohne Schatten* (Flanders), Caliban *Tempest* (ROH/Strasbourg/Lübeck), Sellem *Rake's Progress* (Nantes), Il Primo Sacerdote *Il Prigioniero* (Limoges), Zweiter Junge Offizier *Die Soldaten* (Bochum Ruhrtriennale/Lincoln Centre Festival NYC), Batistelli's *Richard III* (Strasbourg/Geneva), Gerald Barry's *Triumph of Beauty and Deceit* with BCMG (Carnegie Hall). Recent concert performances include *Pulcinella* (Aldeburgh Festival), *Glagolitic Mass* (Brighton Festival), and Rossini's *Stabat Mater* (RTE Concert Orchestra/Israel Sinfonietta). Recordings include the critically acclaimed Ned Rorem *Auden Poems* (Chamber Domaine/Sanctuary Classics) and Michael Berkeley and Ian McEwan's *For You* (MTW/Signum Classics).

Joseph Shovelton *Angel 5 / Porter / Industrialist*
Joseph was born in Leigh, Lancashire, and studied at the Guildhall
School of Music & Drama. He has performed with the D'Oyly Carte
Opera Company, playing the roles of Nanki-Poo, *The Mikado*, Pelegrin
and Armand Brissard *The Count of Luxembourg*, and Ralph, *H.M.S.
Pinafore* at the Savoy Theatre, Royal Festival Hall on UK tour and in the
USA. Previous engagements include Antonio *Duenna* and Trevelyan
One Day, Two Dawns for English Touring Opera. Lippo Fiorentino
Street Scene for The Opera Group at the Young Vic, Watford Palace
Theatre and Buxton Opera House and for Opéra de Toulon, Ingnatz
Krazy Kat for Tête à Tête Opera Festival, Basilio *The Marriage of Figaro*
for Savoy Opera, Marco *The Gondoliers* and Bertie *the Water Babies* at
Chichester Festival; Autumn *The Fairy Queen*, English Bach Festival at
the Linbury Studio. Future performances include a revival of *Street
Scene* for The Opera Group, and Goro *Madame Butterfly* for Opéra de
Toulon in 2012.

Owen Gilhooly *Angel 6 / Gardener / General*
Irish baritone Owen Gilhooly trained with Jean Holmes in Limerick
and Conor Farren in Dublin. He is a graduate of the Royal College of
Music and the National Opera Studio and represented Ireland at the
BBC Cardiff Singer of the World 2007. He has performed extensively
on the operatic platform in Ireland and the UK and in 2009 made
his Viennese debut singing the title role in Conti's *Don Chisciotte in
Serena Morena* for Musikverkstatt Wien. Recent roles include King
Louis XVI *The Ghosts of Versailles* and Lord Salt *The Golden Ticket*
(Wexford Festival), Malatesta *Don Pasquale* (English Touring Opera)
and Figaro *The Barber of Seville* (Stanley Hall Opera). In concert he has
appeared with the RTÉ NSO, Irish Chamber and Ulster Orchestras,
the BBC, Bournemouth and Tokyo Symphony Orchestras, the Royal
Liverpool and London Philharmonic Orchestras and at the BBC
Proms. Future engagements include Albert *Werther* (Les Azuriales
Opera).

Keel Watson *Angel 7 / King*

Keel Watson made his Royal Albert Hall and Barbican debuts in Gershwin's *Porgy and Bess*, and ROH debut as Bosun in *Billy Budd*. Other roles: The King *Aida* (Bregenz), Reinmar *Tannhäuser* (Athens), Fasolt *Das Rheingold* and Creon *Oedipus Rex* (Sao Carlos Theatre, Lisbon), Frazier *Porgy and Bess* (Opera de Lyon and Edinburgh International Festival), Caronte *La favola d'Orfeo* (Opera Zuid and ENO), Elder Ott *Susannah* (Opéra de Nantes), Iago *Othello,* Don Pizarro *Fidelio*, First Apprentice *Wozzeck,* Abbot *Curlew River*, Pluto *Il ballo delle ingrate*, Neptune *Il ritorno d'Ulisse in patria*, Commendatore *Don Giovanni* and Voice of Neptune *Idomeneo* (Birmingham Opera Company), *Don Pasquale* (title role), Dr Bartolo *Le nozze di Figaro*, Colline *La Bohème* (ETO), and Nourabad *Les Pêcheurs de Perles,* Tonio *I pagliacci,* Jorg *Stiffelio* and Bertrand *Iolanta* (Opera Holland Park). For Opera North: Mandryka *Arabella,* the Speaker, Second Armed Man and Second Priest *The Magic Flute,* Zuniga *Carmen.* He appears as Second Armed Man in *The Magic Flute* film directed by Kenneth Branagh.

CREATIVE TEAM

Nicholas Collon *Conductor*

As Artistic Director and Principal Conductor of Aurora Orchestra, Nicholas Collon has performed at the BBC Proms, King's Place, the City of London Festival and the Aldeburgh Festival. Next season he makes his debut with the London Philharmonic Orchestra, Northern Sinfonia and London Mozart Players. Nicholas was the classical music nominee in the Times Breakthrough category at this year's South Bank Sky Arts Awards.

His recent operatic work includes the world premiere of *The Knight Crew* by Julian Phillips for Glyndebourne and Elena Langer's *The Lion's Face* for The Opera Group. He also conducted the first staged opera in the Palestinian Territories with performances of *The Magic Flute* and *La Bohème* in Ramallah and Bethlehem.

Recent engagements include a joint collaboration with the London Sinfonietta and Orchestra of the Age of Enlightenment, a London Symphony Orchestra premiere, recordings with the BBC and BBC Scottish Symphony Orchestras and concerts with Manchester Camerata, Sinfonia Viva and the Orchestra of Opera North. Nicholas' work with Aurora Orchestra currently includes a residency at King's Place, *Mozart Unwrapped,* a continuation of Aurora Orchestra's acclaimed *New Moves* series at LSO St Luke's and a newly released CD of works by Nico Muhly for Decca. Nicholas will also appear at the Bregenz Festival with Symphonieorchester Vorarlberg in a programme of works by Judith Weir.

John Fulljames *Director*

For The Opera Group where he is Artistic Director: *Into the Little Hill, Street Scene, Blond Eckbert, The Nose* and the world premieres of Julian Phillips's *Varjak Paw,* Edward Rushton's *The Shops,* Ed Hughes's *The Birds,* Elena Langer's *The Lion's Face* and Jonathan Dove's *The Enchanted Pig.* Other recent productions include *From the House of the Dead, The Excursions of Mr Brouček, Roméo et Juliette, Saul* and *Hansel and Gretel* (Opera North), *The Portrait* (Bregenz), *Gianni Schicchi, Florentine Tragedy* and *Mavra* (Greek National Opera), *Snegurochka* and *Susannah* (Wexford Festival, winner, Irish Theatre Awards Best Opera Production), *Tobias and the Angel* (Young Vic/ETO) and *Nabucco* (Opera Holland Park).

Tadasu Takamine *Designer*

Tadasu Takamine is an artist with a diverse range of output including performances, videos and installations. His best known works relate to common political subjects such as the imperialistic attitude of the United States, the relationship between sexual ethics and disability, and issues relating to ethnic Koreans in Japan. His works are also marked with personal stories such as hard labour and migration. He often works with his own body to reveal the contradictions and incongruities of the social system that supports constructs such as nation, gender and even language. His works do not shout about politics but aim to voice the problems of power and oppression that result in discrimination and bigotry. His recent activities include theatre direction and stage design where he has moved away from directly dealing with his own body. Whoever's body he is working with, Takamine's works demonstrate a powerful understanding of the human body as an untamed spirit that rejects assimilation into uniformity and of the rich and exuberant communicative state that such a body can offer. His exhibition, *Too Far To See*, is at Ikon Gallery, Birmingham until 17 July 2011.

The Opera Group is grateful to the Daiwa Foundation, Great Britain Sasakawa Foundation and the Japan Foundation for supporting Tadasu Takamine's involvement in *Seven Angels*.

Jon Clark *Lighting Designer*

Opera includes: *The Lion's Face, Into the Little Hill, Recital 1, Down by the Greenwood Side, Street Scene* (The Opera Group); *The Return of Ulysses* (ENO), *Clemency* (ROH2/Scottish Opera); *The Love for Three Oranges* (Scottish Opera/RSAMD); *I Capuleti e I Montecchi, L'Elisir d'Amore, The Barber of Seville, Così Fan Tutte* (Grange Park Opera). Theatre includes: *Hamlet, Greenland, Beauty and the Beast, The Cat in the Hat, Pains of Youth, Our Class* and *Women of Troy* (National Theatre); *King Lear, The Winter's Tale, Silence, The Merchant of Venice* (RSC), *Moonlight, Polar Bears* (Donmar); *Red Bud, Aunt Dan and Lemon, The Pride, Gone Too Far!* (Royal Court); *Into the Woods* (Open Air, Regent's Park); *Been So Long, The Jewish Wife* (Young Vic); *Salome* (Headlong); *The Little Dog Laughed, The Lover & The Collection, Three Days of Rain* – Knight of Illumination Award and Olivier nomination for Best Lighting Design (West End); *The Birthday Party, Spyski!, Water* (Lyric Hammersmith). Dance includes: *Pleasure's Progress* (ROH2); *Clara, Howl, Libera Me, Between the Clock & The Bed* (Bern Ballett); *Lay Me Down Safe, Tenderhook, Sorry for the Missiles* (Scottish Dance Theatre); *Anton & Erin – Cheek to Cheek* (London Coliseum).

Ian William Galloway *Projection Designer*

Ian is a designer, director and filmmaker working with all forms of video for live performance. He has designed theatrically for Frantic Assembly and the National Theatre of Scotland (*Beautiful Burnout*), in the West End (*Flashdance*), Headlong Theatre (*A Midsummer Night's Dream, Medea/Medea*), the Gate Theatre (*The Kreutzer Sonata, Nocturnal*), Nabokov Theatre (*Bunny*), the Royal Shakespeare Company (*The Gods Weep*), The Opera Group (*The Lion's Face*), Udderbelly (*Freerun*), Liverpool Playhouse (*Proper Clever*), the Arcola (*The Spanish Tragedy*), the Royal Court (*Blood*), Complicite (*A Minute Too Late*), South Coast Repertory LA and the Alley Theatre Houston (*Hitchcock Blonde*) and the Nationale Reisopera Netherlands (*Hotel de Pekin*). He has toured the UK, Europe and Japan as a musician, designed and directed projections for concerts (Leona Lewis, Interpol, RizMC) and has directed and produced music videos and shorts. He works as part of Mesmer, a collaboration of video and projection designers working in the fields of theatre, opera, music, art and fashion.

Sandra Maturana *Movement Director*

Sandra is a multilingual actress and director with a strong background in physical theatre. She trained as an actress in Spain and completed an MA at RADA where she specialised in directing. She also attended the Directors Lab at the Lincoln Centre Theatre (NY). As a director she has presented plays at Tara Arts, the Edinburgh Festival and BAC, and she has assisted on several shows including *My Dad's a Birdman* at the Young Vic. Sandra has developed excellent movement skills through her training in different dance disciplines. She has recently worked as a movement director in the parallel production of *The Government Inspector* at the Young Vic. As an actress she has performed in films, dance theatre pieces and experimental theatre. Her credits include *Darkness Cycle* at The Place and playing Tinkerbell in the O2´s production of *Peter Pan*.

Glyn Maxwell

SEVEN ANGELS

Music by Luke Bedford

OBERON BOOKS
LONDON

WWW.OBERONBOOKS.COM

First published in 2011 by Oberon Books Ltd
521 Caledonian Road, London N7 9RH
Tel: +44 (0) 20 7607 3637 / Fax: +44 (0) 20 7607 3629
e-mail: info@oberonbooks.com
www.oberonbooks.com

The vocal or full score and orchestral parts are available from
Luke Bedford (www.universaledition.com/bedford) directly or
through The Opera Group.

A catalogue record for this book is available from the British
Library.

ISBN: 978-1-84943-079-1

Cover design by www.weared8.co.uk

Printed in Great Britain by CPI Antony Rowe, Chippenham.

Characters

THE WAITRESS/1ST ANGEL

THE QUEEN/2ND ANGEL

THE CHEF/THE PRIESTESS/3RD ANGEL

THE PRINCE/4TH ANGEL

THE PORTER/THE INDUSTRIALIST/5TH ANGEL

THE GARDENER/THE GENERAL/6TH ANGEL

THE KING/7TH ANGEL

ACT ONE

THE STORY OF THE ANGELS

(The stars, rising, begin to slow, and come to a standstill. SEVEN ANGELS have fallen to an ashen plain, from which they slowly rise)

ANGELS
So far
    So far
        To fall
So far
    To fall
        It feels
We fall
    It feels
        No more
We find
    No more
        We fall
No more
    We find
        The stars
That rise
    The stars
        That rose
Those stars
    Are still
        Those stars
That rose
    Those stars
        Are still
We too
    Are still
        We too

We rise
       We too
              We rise
Somewhere
       We rise
              Somewhere
A star
       Somewhere
              Is still
A sun
       Is still
              The sun

(The ANGELS stand in the pink early sunlight)

So long we fell
       So long we fell
So long
       So long we fell our names
              So long we fell our names
              Are forgotten
Are forgotten

So long we fell
       So long we fell
              So long
       So long we fell our cause
              So long we fell our cause
                  Is forgotten
              Is forgotten

Now we are still
       Now we are still
              Nowhere
       Now we are still
                     Here
Nowhere
       Now we are still
                     Nowhere

Nowhere
      Nowhere
            Here
                  Here
                       Hear!

(The wind blows, the ANGELS move with it. The day clouds over)

We move
      We move
            What moves us
                  Who moves us
                      Who moves us
                       There
                              There!
                              From there!
                              From there it comes
            What comes
                  Who comes
                       There again
                       From there

Breath
      It breathes
            Breathe
                  Breathe
                              Listen!

A sigh
      A sigh
            What sigh
                It sighs
                  Who sighs
                  It sighs
                       A creature
A creature sighs
      A creature
            The Creature
                              The Creature

(The ANGELS feel raindrops)

A tear
      Tears
            Cries
                 What cries
A tear
      Tears
            Who cries
               Who cries
                   It cries
                           The creature cries
                            The Creature
It is crying
      Why
                              I know why
               Do you know why
It is crying
      Why
           Crying
               Why
                  Crying
                     Why
                              I know why
                              I know why
               Do you know why
                              I know why
                        I know why, I hear
                              I hear
      I hear
                   I hear:
                   Where art thou?
                     Where art thou?
          Where art thou?
             I miss thee here
I miss thee here
      Where art thou?
                   It sighs
                     It cries
                          Where art thou?
              I miss thee here

Who hath
Who hath told thee?

(The wind and rain blow through again, the ANGELS voice what they think it is saying)

WHERE ART THOU?
I MISS THEE HERE
WHO HATH TOLD THEE?

WHERE ART THOU?
I MISS THEE HERE
WHO HATH TOLD THEE?

(The ANGELS cluster together)

Is it we

Are we missed

Are we loved

Is it we

Are we loved

Is it we

No!

No...

(One of the ANGELS begins the story)

Not a creature, a creator...
A creator, then a time...
A better time, if it is crying...
It is deserted...in a desert...

(The other ANGELS start to join in, contemplating the space around them)

If a cry then a creator...
If a sigh, why then a past
Was beautiful and not deserted...
Not a desert but a garden

(A Garden starts to come to life, the day brightens)

If it sighs there was a garden...

If it cries there was a soul
To garden here, there was a soul
To make a garden of a desert

(One of the ANGELS takes the form of a man, the KING)

There was someone who was loved
And in a garden left alone...
But someone loved would not be left
Alone...Someone was in a garden...

(One of the ANGELS takes the form of a woman, the QUEEN)

...*Not* alone, the creature crying
Two are gone who in the past,
Who in a better time were loving
In a garden not a desert

(The KING and QUEEN in their Garden)

Two are gone and not alone
Who in a better time were dear
Who turned a garden to a desert
Who in time turn all to desert
Who in time turn all to desert

Stars rise
Though eyes be closed
Stories stir
The world from dust
Though faces fade
Voices last
Stories stir
The world from dust

(Now it is as if the air itself is bursting to tell stories. The slightest hint or speculation brings something new to life with angelic logic)

If there were two
They made a third
    They made a third
    His name was what?
        His name was all
        There was to see
        His name was SUN

(The sun comes out, brightly, mid-morning yellow, and one of the ANGELS takes the form of a PRINCE)

        They had a son
          If so then loved
            If so then all
            They grew was his
          They loved him so
        They kept nothing
        Nothing from him

(A table. The KING and QUEEN pile the PRINCE's plate with food, and spoil him)

                All they grew
                They grew for him
                All they grew
                They brought to him

Who brought him all
They grew for him?
    We brought him all
    They grew for him
        We came from dust
        From the great desert

2

THE STORY OF THE HOUSEHOLD

(The ANGELS turn to a HOUSEHOLD – an ultra-efficient machine, in which they all harmoniously can do any task – gardening, fetching/carrying, cooking, serving – allowing the KING & QUEEN to do nothing but spoil and caress the PRINCE, and the PRINCE to do nothing but eat)

HOUSEHOLD
We dream we dig
We plough we plant
We reap we raise
    We serve

We make we mill
We sort we store
We test we taste
    We serve

We blend we boil
We roast we roll
We freeze we fry
We serve

KING
A world so fair
That out of heaven
We must have fallen

QUEEN
A world so fair
Where we have fallen
Must be heaven

PRINCE
Mother?

KING
Heaven dear?
A dream of heaven
In a garden

PRINCE
Father?

QUEEN
A dream dear?
This is *our* garden
This is heaven

KING & QUEEN
This is our garden
This is heaven

(The KING and QUEEN leave the PRINCE to it, and go hand in hand to a shady spot where they will make their Garden. Meanwhile the ANGELS form a perfect HOUSEHOLD with no complaints. Then their logic takes hold)

ANGELS
And what of him
    Who never went
        Without a thing?
    He went without
Some thing
    He went without
        Some thing...

                PRINCE
                Father?
                Pa! Pa!
                Mother?
                Ma? Ma?
                More! More!

(The PRINCE's needs make the HOUSEHOLD move faster. The ANGELS jump to it, diverging into four distinct roles: the GARDENER harvests the crop, the PORTER brings the produce in, the CHEF makes the meals, and the WAITRESS serves the meals to the PRINCE)

GARDENER	PORTER	CHEF	WAITRESS
I grow			
	I store		
		I make	
			I serve
I grow			
I gather	I store		
	I carry	I make	
		I master	I wait
PRINCE			I serve
More! More!			

(On they work, occasionally stepping out of the machine to make their feelings known)

                CHEF
                I love to cook for him
                Who's never even known my name...

PRINCE

More!

PORTER

I love to mind the store
I'm sure it's all my life is for

PRINCE

More!

GARDENER

Oh I love to weed the earth
God knows it's all my time is worth

PRINCE

More!

WAITRESS

More, more, he will eat so much
When he bursts I'll burst with laughter!
More, more, he will grow so fat
His voice won't even reach me!
More, more, I could be the moon
Or a star that he can wish on!
More! More? I'm so far away
I'm gone before you see me
More, more, I'm so far away
I'm gone before you see me

(The KING and QUEEN have ceased to work, and recline on thrones. By now the PRINCE is growing extremely corpulent. The HOUSEHOLD still functions, albeit under strain)

PRINCE

More...More...More...

(The PRINCE sleeps, with his face in his plate. The HOUSEHOLD turn back into fatigued ANGELS)

3

THE STORY OF THE GARDEN

(The KING and QUEEN are looking upon the Garden with glazed admiration)

ANGELS
And what of those
Whose son he was?
    His father?
    His mother?
        All they saw
        As he grew and grew
    Was wealth
    Was power
Until he grew so vast
Clouds formed on him – the son
Was hidden, and they turned
With pride towards their Garden

    (The sun climbs towards noon. As the KING and QUEEN observe the rainbow
    colours of the Garden, each colour brightens intensely in turn)

QUEEN
The only Heaven
Our Garden

KING
Yes the only Heaven
Our Garden!
– Violet
The glory

        QUEEN
        Our glory
        That we alone were chosen

KING
Indigo
The mystery

        QUEEN
        Our mystery
        That silence surrounds us

KING
Blue
The endless

QUEEN
Our endless
Palisade of sunlight

KING
Green
The new life

QUEEN
Our new life
Prospering at our pleasure

KING
Gold
The riches here

QUEEN
Our riches
Blossoming ever further

KING
Orange
The harvest

QUEEN
Our harvest
Never ending summer

KING
Red
The power

QUEEN
Our power
To keep, now and forever

(The KING and QUEEN sing a hymn of praise to the Garden)

KING & QUEEN
What all desire
Is only here
Mercy and plenty and peace, O
All that is well
All that can heal
Is flowering in this place, O

(The wind rises, taking the hymn to the Ends of the Earth)

ANGELS
Surely the world
Could hear the song?
Surely the wind
Ran round the world?

> *(Three silhouettes appear – BENIGHTED SOULS hearing the hymn in their dreams)*

To one who starves in the north
> *Plenty...*

> **To one who wanders the south**

Peace...

> **And to one in despair very far from here**
> **Where the sun bites into the earth**
> > *Mercy...*

> *(The KING is still humming the tune, but the QUEEN stops him suddenly)*

QUEEN
Sing no more
For all will hear

KING
But all the world
Deserves to know!

QUEEN
All the world
Come trampling here?
No – No
Lock the gate and raise the wall
The Garden is too beautiful
Too vulnerable too valuable
To see at all

> *(The KING still dithers)*

QUEEN
Are you a King?
If not then who?
Who are you?

KING

We have grown enough
We have given enough
Now it's ours

Enough
Enough
Ours

And no one else's	No one else's
All can eat	Enough
From the palace stores	Enough
The world outside	Ours
Can stuff their faces	No one else's
For others	Enough
There will always be enough	Enough
There'll never be enough	Ours
For you	Me
Me	You
Me	Me

(The KING becomes helpless in the face of pleasure and makes a decision)

Lock the gate and raise the wall
The Garden is too beautiful
Too vulnerable too valuable
To see at all

(The KING and QUEEN bar the gates to the Garden, and get to it. The Wall blocks the Garden from our sight, the day clouds over and the wind blows)

4

THE STORY OF THE PRINCE

(The GARDENER comes to fetch fresh produce from the Garden but finds the gate barred, and a faint light emanating from there)

GARDENER
The Garden is closed!

PORTER
The Garden is closed?
The Garden is closed!

CHEF
The Garden is closed?
Now nothing's fresh!
And every meal
Is one meal less

PORTER
But every meal
He asks for more
And the sun sinks
On the palace store

GARDENER
No rest at all
And pay? what pay?
Hungrier hungrier
Day by day

CHEF	**PORTER**	**GARDENER**	
The Garden closed?			
Now nothing's fresh!	But every meal		
And every meal	He asks for more	**GARDENER**	
Is one meal less	And the sun sinks	No rest at all	
The Garden closed!	On the palace store	And pay? What pay?	

CHEF	**PORTER**	**GARDENER**	**WAITRESS**
The Garden closed!	The Garden closed!	Hungrier hungrier	What will we grow
		Day by day	We will grow weak
The Garden closed!	The Garden closed!	The Garden closed!	Hungrier hungrier
			Week by week

HOUSEHOLD
Month by month
Year by year
Generation
By generation

PRINCE

I hear sad songs
I too am sad!
My plate is almost
Empty, I almost
See myself! So...
Bring me more!
More! More!

(The WAITRESS hurries away)

PRINCE

Where have you gone?
You have gone away
Everyone everyone
Goes from me

(The WAITRESS comes back with more, and he falls to eating, singing with his mouth full)

PRINCE

More comes too slow
Not quick enough
Not soon enough!
Help her to bring more!
The gardener, the gardener!

(The WAITRESS runs to the GARDENER, who has had enough)

GARDENER

Oh I love to weed the earth
God knows it's all my time was worth

(The GARDENER gives the WAITRESS his gloves, and leaves. Struggling with twice as much to do, she runs back to the PRINCE, who continues, as ever, to eat with his back turned)

PRINCE

Gardener, gardener,
Help her to bring more!

WAITRESS-AS-GARDENER

Oh I love to weed the earth
God knows it's all my time was worth

PRINCE

Gardener you smell so sweet
You're supposed to smell of earth
You always smell of earth

WAITRESS-AS-GARDENER

Prince it is the fashion
At the foot of a thousand stairs
To eat the petals from the roses
When there's nothing else

PRINCE

More comes too slow
Not soon enough
Not food enough!
Help them to bring more!
The porter! The porter!

(The WAITRESS runs to the PORTER, who has had enough)

PORTER

I love to mind the store
I'm sure it's all my life is for

(The PORTER gives the WAITRESS his apron, and leaves. She runs back to the PRINCE, who continues, as ever, to eat with his back turned)

PRINCE

Porter, porter,
Bring more, bring more!

WAITRESS-AS-PORTER

Oh I love to mind the store
I'm sure it's all my life is for

PRINCE

Porter you have a light voice

47

You're meant to have a dark voice
You always had a dark voice

WAITRESS-AS-PORTER
Prince it is the fashion
At the foot of a thousand stairs
Barely to have the strength to speak
Voices are small there

PRINCE
More comes too slow
Not soon enough
Not food enough
Help them to make more!
The Chef! The Chef!

(The WAITRESS runs to the CHEF, who has had enough)

CHEF
I love to cook for him
Who's never even known my name!

*(The CHEF gives the WAITRESS her hat, and leaves. Now the WAITRESS has to be
CHEF too, and it's just too much. She sinks to the floor, and weeps with exhaustion. Three
ANGELS – who had been the rest of the Household – gather round her)*

(The PRINCE gets to the end of his meal, and sees his own face in the empty plate)

PRINCE
Whose are these eyes?
Whose is this opening
Opening mouth?
Whose are these teeth
These tombs in red earth?
I can see myself
Why can I see
Myself?
Chef?
Chef?
Why can I see myself?

5

THE STORY OF THE WAITRESS

ANGELS
And what of her
      Who *was* she?
            One of us?
      Who *was* she?
No one saw her
      One of us?
            No one loved her
      One of us
No more
      She does not know
            No more
      She does not know us
Instead of knowing –
      Love came
            Instead of knowing –
      Love came

PRINCE
Why is my plate
Empty?

WAITRESS-AS-CHEF
We were late
We were slow
There were not enough of us
On earth for you

PRINCE
      But I
Can see you I
Can see you – you –
Chef you have a sweet face
It was usually an ugly face
In my mind it was an ugly face
But now you have a sweet face

WAITRESS-AS-CHEF

Prince it is the fashion
At the foot of a thousand stairs
To be as we were made, no more
So there, so there

PRINCE

      I can
See you, but why?
I can see you in my plate
Don't look at me

WAITRESS-AS-CHEF

      I am not
Looking at you

PRINCE

Don't look at me

WAITRESS-AS-CHEF

      I am not
Looking at you I am
Looking at your plate
I am feeding you

(The WAITRESS is serving him, but he has turned from his plate to look at her in the world)

PRINCE

I can see you in the room
I can see you there
You are not the Gardener, are you,
The Porter, the Chef, you are
Not anyone I know
Have you always looked like that?

WAITRESS

See me
Can you?
There is no one left
I am all that's left
I make I bake I fry I filet
I dice I chop I shell I sautée
I batter I burn I weep I weep
I do what you want
I do not stop

PRINCE

Why is there only you?

WAITRESS

Hear me
Can you?
They are gone away
All gone away

PRINCE

My arm can throw a shadow
Wide as all your body
But I don't wish to hide you
Not see you
Not see you
Rest now
Here now
There now

(The PRINCE lets her sit)

WAITRESS

We must go to your father's Garden

PRINCE

It is a forbidden Garden!

WAITRESS

Food was grown there in the past
The palace stores are failing fast
We must go to your father's Garden

PRINCE

It is a sacred Garden!

WAITRESS

Every seed of every flower
Every nut of every fruit
Was safe there, was alive there
We must open your father's Garden

PRINCE

Who are we to see the Garden?

WAITRESS

You could not see me
Your eyes were closed
You see me now
And your eyes are bright
Open your father's Garden
Open what you think is closed
And you can eat

PRINCE

      And I can eat...

WAITRESS

And you can eat

PRINCE

      And I can eat!

WAITRESS

And I can eat

PRINCE

    And you can eat

WAITRESS

Ha!

(She has tricked him into saying that, but now he listens to what he said, looks at her and considers the implications)

PRINCE

And...*you*...can eat...
And...*you*...can eat...

WAITRESS

And we can eat

PRINCE

    And...*we*...can eat...

WAITRESS

And they can eat

PRINCE

    And...*who*?

(He is staring at her)

WAITRESS

Never mind, it's a start
A seed, a nut, an acorn
Everything starts somewhere
You were once a tiny child
And I was once a happy one
And everything starts somewhere
We shall open your father's garden
We shall open your father's garden
What are you looking at?
Rise up out of your seat,
You planet, out of your orbit,
This is no time to drool at the moon
This is the time for – *something*!

(For the first time in ages, the PRINCE rises and they go together towards the Garden, from which a dazzling light and a humming noise now emanate)

PRINCE AND WAITRESS
What all desire
Is only there
Mercy and plenty and peace, O
All that is well
All that can heal
Is flowering in that place, O

(They become ANGELS once more)

ANGELS
Surely the world
Could hear the song
Surely the wind
Ran round the world

On the wind a man is riding
Who is master of all nature
Who has harvested all matter
Wealthy man who dwells in desert

(We see a VISION OF THE NORTH. Blown forward by the wind, an INDUSTRIALIST staggers along. Images on the screen of post-industrial desolation)

INDUSTRIALIST
My realm is dust
My people starve
A plentiful garden
Is all I dream of

ANGELS
Up against the wind a soldier
Who will fight with all he faces
Who will march this world to battle
Violent man who lives by fire

(We see a VISION FROM THE SOUTH. Fighting the wind in his face, a GENERAL stumbles along. Images on the screen of torn cities and refugees)

GENERAL
War sears my land
To blackened space
Of a garden I dream
Of endless peace

ANGELS
In the moonlight walks a priestess
With her book and with her sword
But when the moonlight turns its back
The world is nothing but Her Word

(The clouds break and the moon rises. We see a VISION FROM THE EAST, a PRIESTESS walking in moonlight. Images on the screen of preachers, books burning, millions marching in step)

PRIESTESS
Fear and despair
Are the masters there
But a merciful garden
Draws me here

(The VISIONS fade)

WAITRESS & PRINCE
What all desire
Is only here
Mercy and plenty and peace, O
All that is well
All that can heal
Is flowering in this place, O

(The PRINCE tries the barred gate of the Garden and it swings open, broken, revealing – a jungle of dead plants. The walls have blocked so much light that everything has died. The light and sound are coming from malfunctioning, familiar machinery. The QUEEN is drunkenly singing, The KING is trying to plant a tiny tree in a tiny plot)

QUEEN

La la la la
La la la la
La la la
La la la

(Blackout)

ACT TWO

6

THE STORY OF THE CONFERENCE

(It is TODAY. There is a great table laid for the Conference. There are places set for six, each with excessively complex cutlery and huge ring-binder files. The WAITRESS is despondently leafing through the PRINCE's file)

WAITRESS
Nothing
Come to nothing
Hope all hope all
Come to nothing
Nothing is growing
Nothing is spreading
Nothing is coming
Come to nothing
A harvest of nothing

PRINCE
The stores
The palace stores!

WAITRESS
A year and a day
A year? A day?
At the most
Then dust
Then nothing
Nothing

> *(The WAITRESS weeps. The PRINCE wants to console her, but he can't reach her on account of his girth)*

PRINCE
What are you weeping for?
Rise up out of your tears,
You ocean, out of despair,
This is no time to water the dust
This is the time for – *something*!

WAITRESS
There's nothing we can do

PRINCE
       No!
For you, for you
I shall be as I was before
I shall ask for *more* More!

WAITRESS
O hopeless fat fool

PRINCE
No!
I shall ask for *more* More!
Then...take a bite...and then
I shall send it back to you
And you shall eat

WAITRESS *(getting it)*
       And...I shall eat...
A bite...and then I shall –
Take it to the palace gate
And *they* shall eat

PRINCE
       And they shall eat?
And they shall eat!

WAITRESS
And all shall eat

PRINCE
And my mother will know nothing
And my father will know nothing

WAITRESS
And secretly the world will eat,
The starving of the north
The homeless of the south
The hunted of the east
But how will it be enough?
It will never be enough

PRINCE
Nothing is not enough
To do nothing is not enough
O hopeless skinny fool!

(The KING and QUEEN arrive from one side to greet the DELEGATES arriving from the other. There is the INDUSTRIALIST of the North, the GENERAL of the South, the PRIESTESS of the East. There are places set for each of them. The WAITRESS takes from the guests their enormous coats and is buried beneath them, till she is as encumbered as the PRINCE)

INDUSTRIALIST
My realm is dust
My people starve
A plentiful garden
All I dream of

GENERAL
War sears my land
To blackened space
Of a garden I dream
Of endless peace

PRIESTESS
Fear and despair
Are the masters there
But a merciful garden
Draws me here

INDUSTRIALIST/GENERAL/PRIESTESS
What all desire
Is only here
Mercy and plenty and peace, O
All that is well
All that can heal
Is flowering in this place, O

This hymn was heard
At the ends of the world
In all our dreams
At the ends of the world
This hymn was heard
And it drew us here
May we see this heavenly Garden?
May we come to this green haven?

PRINCE
Mother what will you tell them?

QUEEN
You think you have seen the Garden
But there is a secret Garden
I have seen it in a vision
In my vision they are working
On a new eternal Garden
New ideas
New thinking
In their millions
They are working
Far as the eye can see
Far as the eye can see
An infinity of plenty

(The KING opens his folder)

KING
First on the agenda
And we must have an agenda
First we must have breakfast!

(The DELEGATES take their place at the table)

(As the QUEEN announces the Breakfast Menu, the WAITRESS – doing the work of chef, porter, gardener and waitress – is in perpetual motion)

QUEEN
Bellini pecan hollandaise
Frittata citrus apple-smoked
Asparagus chorizo hash
Manchego muesli mushroom latte
Bloody mary bloody mary

(The KING, QUEEN and DELEGATES eat and drink heartily)

PRINCE
Disgusting!
I can't touch that!
Something else! More! More!

QUEEN *(to the WAITRESS)*
Fool, fool, he gets what he wants
So get what he wants
And get it at once
For as far as the eye can see
Is an infinity of plenty

(The WAITRESS takes the rejected food from the PRINCE, hurries down to the kitchen, and sets it outside the back door of the palace)

KING
Now my brother from the North
What on earth is on your mind?

(The INDUSTRIALIST rises. What's on his mind is shown on the screen. The DELEGATES eat)

INDUSTRIALIST
Forging of metals burning of sea-coal
Great stink great smog greenfield brownfield
Sulphur dioxide particulate matter
Eutrophication wastewater discharge
Herbicide pesticide actinide litter
Chemical critical chromium cadmium
Gasoline benzene toxin dioxin
Arsenic incineration ozone acid
     Seed into ashes

Seed into ashes
I stood by an ocean solid and burning
Could barely catch my
Barely catch my
Show us your Garden
Your plentiful Garden

(The only sound is the KING turning the pages of his folder)

KING
Thank you...thank you...
Marvellous...
It is very much so
Oh very much so...
Ah, next on the agenda
And we must have an agenda
Next we must have luncheon!

(The DELEGATES can't help but notice there is not so much on offer this time, despite what the QUEEN is saying)

QUEEN
Caramelised crostini crème
Balsamic blackened boeuf purée
Horseradish remoulade pancetta
Glazed meringue shiitake feta
Chateau Lafitte Chateau Lafitte!

(The KING, QUEEN and DELEGATES eat and drink heartily)

PRINCE
Disgusting!
I can't touch that!
Something else! More! More!

QUEEN
Fool, fool, he gets what he wants
So get what he wants
And get it at once
For as far as the eye can see
Is an infinity of plenty

(The WAITRESS takes the rejected food from the PRINCE, hurries down to the kitchen, and sets it outside the back door of the palace)

KING
Now my brother from the South
What on earth is on your mind?

(The GENERAL rises. What's on his mind is shown on the screen. The DELEGATES eat)

GENERAL
Pride in principle discipline pack-drill
Militant crackdown criminal national
Borderline skirmish outrage avenge us
Hundreds and millions glory glory
Invasion insurgency genocide stronghold
Rebel horizon rape to a backbeat
Compound encampment infection starvation
Asylum the rain on a railway nowhere
      Brother and sister
      Brother and sister
Not on the list when the list is the living
      I don't see their names
      I don't see their names
Show us your Garden
Your peaceable Garden

(The only sound is the KING turning the pages of his folder)

KING
Thank you...thank you...
Tremendous...
Very much so
It is very much so...
Ah, next on the agenda
And we must have an agenda
Next we must have supper!

(Nothing happens)

QUEEN

Next we must take supper!

(Nothing happens)

QUEEN

Waitress! WAITRESS!

(The WAITRESS appears, close to exhaustion)

QUEEN

You are making us WAIT, waitress!

WAITRESS

I am doing all I can

PRINCE

She is doing all she can!

QUEEN

Who said that? Who said that?

(The PRINCE loses his nerve)

QUEEN

Gardener! Porter! Chef!

WAITRESS

They can hear you, Majesty,
And we all feel the same
We are doing all we can
We are bringing all there is

QUEEN

You are failing! You are failing!

PRINCE

Let her be!

QUEEN

Who said that?

(The PRINCE loses his nerve again)

QUEEN
Girl, bring the guests their supper!
From the very ends of the earth they come!
The very ends of the earth!

(The WAITRESS goes)

KING
Now my sister from the East
What on earth is on your mind?

(The PRIESTESS rises. What's on her mind is shown on the screen. The DELEGATES eat)

PRIESTESS
The word and the word and the word and the word
Is, was, will be, so be it so be it
Miracle marvel believer betrayer
Flesh of my blood of my flesh of my blood of my
Light bright heat hot answer the question
Heretic infidel infinite mercy
Mercy mercy past understanding
The word and the will and the blood and the question
    Thy will be done to
    Thy will be done to
Found in a church were a thousand lying
    Murdered at prayer
    Murdered at prayer
Show us your Garden
Your merciful Garden

(The KING turns the pages of his folder, and the QUEEN pours herself the last wine in the world)

KING
Thank you...thank you...
Inspiring...
Very much so
It is very much so...
Now where's my agenda...
Any news on that supper?

(The QUEEN announces the supper menu – but this time no one comes)

QUEEN
Turbot tartare mignonette
Softshell iceberg roasted Caesar
Shark-fin dolphin dauphinoise
Caviar lobster fois gras fondue

(The WAITRESS trundles the trolley in with a few mouldy vegetables and mugs of water on it)

QUEEN
Champagne! Champagne!
Krug! KRUG!
KRUUUUUUUUUUG!

(Silence falls on this animal cry)

WAITRESS
There is no more
There is no more

QUEEN
Liar! Liar! You are hiding it hoarding it
Liar! Liar! You are dining devouring
Liar! Liar!

PRINCE
Enough!

QUEEN
Who said that?
Who said that?

PRINCE
Enough!
Enough!

(The PRINCE, lean and fit, emerges from his corpulent old body, in time to defend the WAITRESS)

PRINCE

Every meal you eat so much
Is a thousand meals you eat so much
And every plate you steal from them
Is a thousand plates you steal from them
A year went by while you gorged yourselves
A year and a day went by and I
I am your son
Who is no one
Who had everything
While no one
Had anything

PRINCE & WAITRESS

We are done
We are man and woman born
And we are starving

(The QUEEN collapses in horror)

INDUSTRIALIST	**GENERAL**	**PRIESTESS**
Show us your Garden	Show us your Garden	Show us your Garden
Your plentiful Garden	Your peaceable Garden	Your merciful Garden

(The KING sinks in despair)

WAITRESS

What will you tell the hungry now
There are no meals to feed them?
What will you tell your people now
There are no tales to tell them?

QUEEN

Far as the eye can see
Is an infinity of plenty

| **INDUSTRIALIST** | **GENERAL** | **PRIESTESS** |
| An infinity of plenty? | An infinity of plenty? | An infinity of plenty? |

(The PRINCE goes to the curtains concealing the Garden and throws them open to reveal an exact model of THEMSELVES, seven of them, the table, the ring-binders, like a doll's house version of the stage. The tiny Prince in the model is frozen at the moment he is opening the curtains to reveal an even smaller version, as if this dwindles into ever smaller versions of the same thing. The QUEEN's 'infinity' is merely the endless reflection of themselves)

(The QUEEN sinks to the ground. The KING curls up in a ball)

QUEEN
Far as the eye can see

WAITRESS & PRINCE
We are all the Garden was
We are all the Garden is

(The DELEGATES let out a long serpentine hiss, the hiss rises into the wind, the wind bends the tree backwards, then rises and rises, blowing the pages from every ring-binder so that blank paper is blown everywhere. Everything is blown away but SEVEN ANGELS)

7

THE STORY OF THE STARS

(The stars appear)

ANGELS
(WAITRESS)   **(PRINCE)**
Ssss...
    Ssss...
        Ssss...
Sssh...   **Sshh**...
    Shhh...   Hush...
      Hush   No more
No more   **Nowhere**   No more
    No more   No matter
      No matter   No matter
Who was I   **Who**   Who was
    Hush   Was I
      Who I   I was
     Who was I   Was I who
Was I   Hush
      No more
     Was I   No matter
Hush
I was   Hush   Hush
     Hush
     Was I   Hush
Was I

(The PRINCE-ANGEL and WAITRESS-ANGEL are trying to remember, to recognise each other, but the other five ANGELS come around them as if to heal them of this. The stars begin to rise)

WAITRESS	PRINCE	ANGELS
	I see you	Hush
I am not		Hush
Looking at you	I see you, can you	Hush
	See me	No more
Can you		Nowhere
See me, can you		No matter
Hear me		Hush
	Can you	Hush
		Hush
No more		No more
	Nowhere	Nowhere
No matter	No matter	No matter
No more	No more	No more

(The WAITRESS and the PRINCE are fading back into ANGELS. The stars are rising now)

WAITRESS	PRINCE	ANGELS
No more	No more	No more
No more	No more	No more
No more	No more	No more

(The WAITRESS remembers)

WAITRESS	PRINCE	ANGELS
More!		
	More?	
More!		No more
You were		
You were		Nowhere
A prince		
	A prince?	
	A prince	No matter
	And you	
	You brought me	
Food		
So you could eat		
	So I could eat	
So you could eat		

                        So I could eat
So I could eat

                        So you could eat
So we could eat   So we could eat
So they could eat   So they could eat
                Out there
                Out there
                Out there
                Where we are
                The stars are still
                The stars are real

                We do not fall
                The world is here
                The sun
                The sun is low
                The hour is late

                We do
                We do not fall
                The world is here
                The sun is low
                The hour is late

                The sun is low
                The hour is late

(The sun is low but not setting, rising. The morning light reveals a desolate landscape, and what seemed to be stars are in fact campfires on the hills – people from everywhere. The PRINCE and the WAITRESS turn to see them. Hand in hand they set off towards them, dwindling to two lights lost among them)

        *   *   *   *   *   *   *